How Your Body Works

Controlling
the Blood

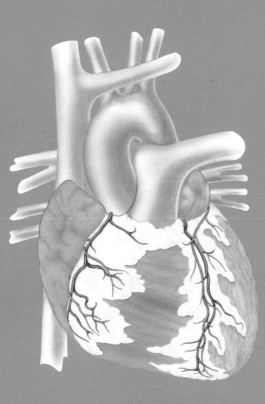

by Penny Preston

AMICUS

Published by Amicus
P.O. Box 1329, Mankato, Minnesota 56002

Printed in the United States of America, at Corporate Graphics
in North Mankato, Minnesota

Library of Congress Cataloging-in-Publication Data
Preston, Penny.
  Controlling the blood / by Penny Preston.
      p. cm. -- (How your body works)
  Includes index.
  Summary: "Discusses blood and its role in functioning and protecting the body"--Provided by publisher.
  ISBN 978-1-60753-051-0 (lib. bdg.)
  1. Blood--Juvenile literature. I. Title.
  QP91.P727 2011
  612.1'1--dc22
                                              2009031778

Created by Appleseed Editions Ltd.
Designed by Helen James
Edited by Mary-Jane Wilkins and Pip Morgan
Artwork by Graham Rosewarne
Picture research by Su Alexander

Photograph acknowledgements
page 5 Edelmann/Science Photo Library; 6 Photo Insolite Realite/Science Photo Library;
7 & 8 Steve Gschmeissner/Science Photo Library; 9 Porterfield-Chickering/Science Photo Library;
13 Roger Cracknell 05/London/Alamy; 15 Sean Aidan; Eye Ubiquitous/Corbis; 17t Science Photo
Library, b Steve Gschmeissner/Science Photo Library; 19 Mika/Zefa/Corbis; 21 Geoff Tomkinson/
Science Photo Library; 22 Martin Philbey/Zuma/Corbis; 23 Sheila Terry/Science Photo Library;
25 Martin Dohrn/Royal College of Surgeons/Science Photo Library; 27 Alain Pol, ISM/Science
Photo Library; 28 BSIP/VEM/Science Photo Library; 29 Faye Norman/Science Photo Library
Front cover Photo Insolite Realite/Science Photo Library

DAD0037
32010

9 8 7 6 5 4 3 2 1

Contents

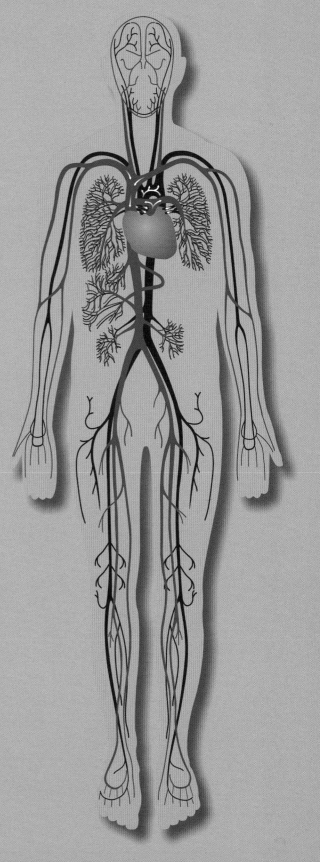

Blood Is Crucial

When you cut yourself and see the drops of blood,
it's hard to imagine how important this red liquid is.
Your blood keeps you alive as it moves through your body.
Every cell in your body needs blood to fetch and carry
chemicals, to fight off infections, and to heal wounds.

What's in Your Blood?

Your blood has billions of tiny cells that float in a watery, pale yellow liquid called **plasma**. There are three main types of blood cells—red cells, white cells, and **platelets**—and each has a different job.

Red blood cells are shaped like doughnuts. They pick up oxygen from your lungs and deliver it to every cell in your body. White blood cells fight germs that cause infections. Platelets are the tiniest of all—they help to form the **clots** that stop bleeding when you cut yourself.

Blood plasma is mostly water mixed with **nutrients** from food and other useful things. Plasma also carries waste products away from the cells and takes them to the liver and kidneys, which get rid of them.

More than half your blood is a liquid called plasma, which is mostly water.

Almost half of your blood contains cells that are invisible to the naked eye.

Checking the Balance

The major **organs** of your body make sure that your blood is carefully checked. The lungs make sure the blood is carrying enough oxygen and not too much carbon dioxide, and the kidneys keep the level of water right. The marrow inside your bones makes every kind of blood cell whenever they're needed. Your liver and kidneys help to get rid of waste products, which might poison your blood. Your heart acts like a pump, making sure that your blood flows at just the right speed. Finally, your **nervous system** controls the force of blood against the walls of your **arteries** as it moves around your body. This is called your **blood pressure**.

In the Womb

When a baby is in the womb, its mother's blood brings the baby everything it needs. Blood passes from mother to baby through the placenta and umbilical cord, carrying oxygen and nutrients. Once the baby's cells have used the oxygen and made waste products, the blood flows back to the mother for more oxygen and nutrients.

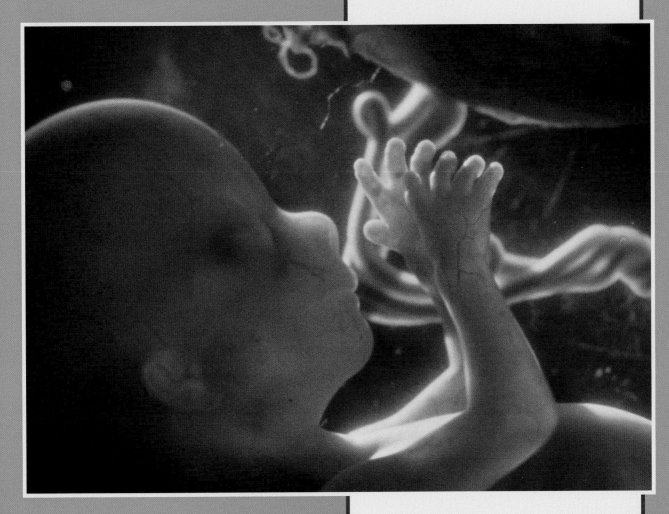

What's in Your Blood?

Your blood is full of things that keep you alive. It contains three types of blood cells (red cells, white cells, and platelets) as well as chemicals that travel to and from the cells in different parts of your body.

A close-up photo of human red blood cells.

Carrying Oxygen

Your blood has more red cells than any other type—just under half the total. These cells are shaped like doughnuts and contain a chemical called **hemoglobin**. This carries oxygen from your lungs and also gives blood its color. Every cell lives for about 120 days before it is scrapped by your liver. A jelly inside your bones called **bone marrow** makes new blood cells—about three million of them every minute!

Fighting Germs

For every 800 red cells, your blood has one white blood cell. These are part of your body's defense system and protect

A colored and magnified photo of white blood cells and smaller (dark blue) platelets.

it from infections. Most white blood cells are killer cells that swallow germs, disease cells, and other unwanted objects in your blood. Others act like disinfectants and make chemicals that attack and destroy harmful materials. White blood cells can live for a few days or as long as a few weeks.

Plugging Holes

Platelets are not complete cells, but tiny scraps of cells that help to plug holes in blood vessels—for example, if you cut yourself. They rush to where the cut is and patch it up so that the bleeding stops. The patch they make on the outside of your body is called a scab (see pages 8–9).

Special Protection

Immunizations can protect you from some illnesses, such as measles and mumps. They are usually given to you in injections. One kind of immunization contains lots of ready-made antibodies that attack the illness if it enters your blood. Another kind triggers your white cells to produce their own antibodies and fight off the illness.

Blood Groups

There are four main blood groups: A, B, AB, and O. Most people belong to the O group. You can donate some of your blood for people who need it, but it will only help them if it's safe to mix your blood type with theirs.

7

Bleeding and Clotting

When you cut yourself, your blood immediately starts to form a plug, which blocks the hole in the damaged blood vessel. This plug doesn't last long and is soon replaced by a scab. All this is made possible by the tiny blood cell scraps called platelets. The platelets form the first plug and then begin to make the stronger and harder scab.

Clots and Scabs

When you damage a blood vessel, the platelets in your blood become sticky and quickly clump together to stop the bleeding. Within a couple of seconds, the blood vessel also grows narrower so less blood can flow through it. The platelets release chemicals that trigger

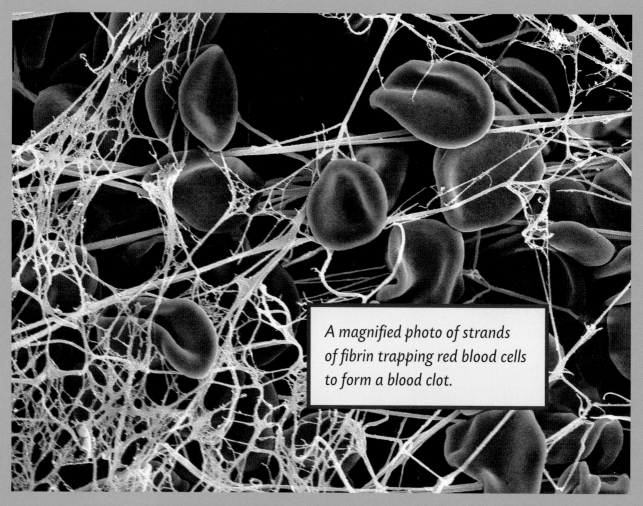

A magnified photo of strands of fibrin trapping red blood cells to form a blood clot.

How a Cut Heals

Blood escapes through cut.

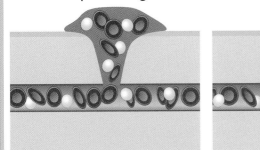

Platelets rush to blood in cut to help plug hole.

Scab forms to protect skin cells mending underneath.

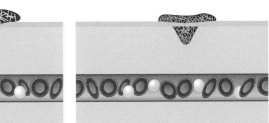

a series of reactions. These help to form a mesh of strands that traps red blood cells and forms a clot. As more strands grow and trap more blood cells, the clot becomes harder and gradually dries to form a hard scab. New skin grows underneath the scab. When this new skin is ready, the scab falls off.

WHEN THINGS GO WRONG

Problem Blood

If one of the chemicals needed for a clot to form is missing, the blood will not clot properly. People who have hemophilia don't have a chemical called factor VIII in their blood. This means they bleed and bruise very easily. The bleeding can be controlled if they have regular injections of the missing clotting factor.

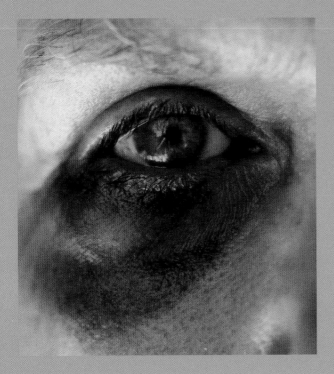

Bruising and Black Eyes

When you injure yourself, blood can leak from tiny blood vessels under the skin to form a bruise. A black eye is caused by blood collecting under the skin around the eye. Bruises change color as the hemoglobin in the blood breaks down.

Blood has collected under the skin to form a bruise in this black eye.

Making New Cells

Red blood cells, most white blood cells, and platelets all develop in the bone marrow inside many of the bones in your body. All cells begin as simple stem cells that can grow into any type of cell—for example, a blood cell, a muscle cell, or a nerve cell.

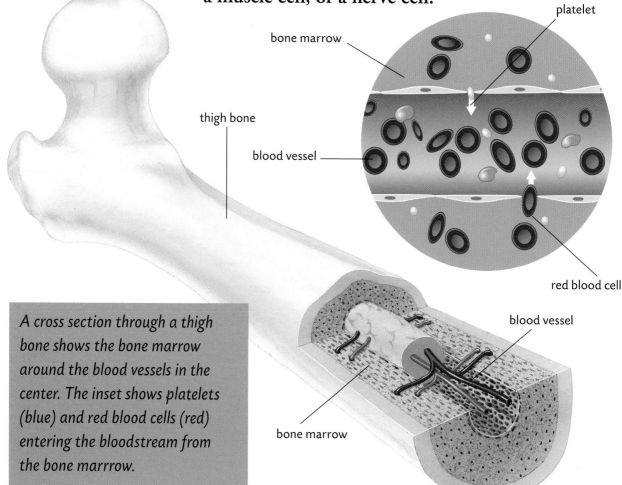

platelet

bone marrow

thigh bone

blood vessel

red blood cell

blood vessel

bone marrow

A cross section through a thigh bone shows the bone marrow around the blood vessels in the center. The inset shows platelets (blue) and red blood cells (red) entering the bloodstream from the bone marrrow.

Adults grow blood cells mainly in their flat bones, such as the ribs and skull, as well as in the upper part of the long bones in their arms and legs. Children grow blood cells in the marrow of most bones in their bodies.

What Happens to Old Cells?

Red blood cells live for about 120 days before they are scrapped and broken down by the liver, **spleen**, and bone marrow. A **hormone** made by the kidneys makes sure that the bone marrow grows the same number of new red cells as the number that are scrapped. The hemoglobin from the scrapped red blood cells is turned into a chemical called **bilirubin**, which is broken down by the liver (see pages 24–25). White blood cells last between a few days and a few weeks before they too are broken down in the liver and spleen.

Bone Marrow Transplants

Sometimes the body's bone marrow develops abnormal cells, for example, when someone has cancer. When this happens, they need to be replaced with cells from a healthy **donor**. First the abnormal cells are destroyed, often by drugs. Then about a liter of bone marrow may be taken from the hip bone of the donor and transplanted into one of the patient's veins. The new cells travel in the bloodstream to where the bone marrow is made around the body, where they multiply to form many normal blood cells.

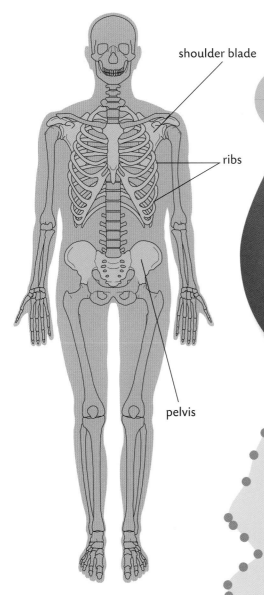

shoulder blade

ribs

pelvis

Adults make blood cells in the bones of the ribs, pelvis, and shoulder blades.

Did You Know?

Your body probably makes and destroys about two million red blood cells every second.

WHEN THINGS GO WRONG

Not Enough Red Blood Cells

People whose bodies don't make enough red blood cells or break down the cells too quickly don't have enough red cells in their blood. This gives them **anemia**. If the number of red cells in their blood falls too low, these people may become out-of-breath and very tired because not enough oxygen reaches their tissues.

Traveling Around

Blood is carried to every part of your body by a branching network of blood vessels. There are three main types of blood vessels —arteries, veins, and the millions of tiny **capillaries** that connect them.

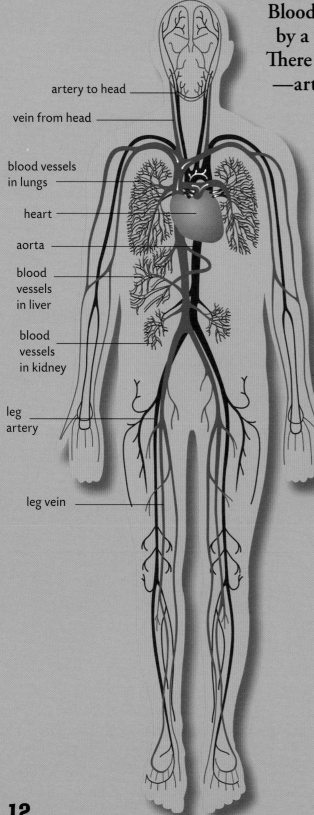

artery to head

vein from head

blood vessels in lungs

heart

aorta

blood vessels in liver

blood vessels in kidney

leg artery

leg vein

From Large to Small

The biggest artery in the body is the **aorta**, which leaves the left side of the heart and then branches into narrower arteries. These eventually come to the tiniest vessels of all, the capillaries. At $1/1000$ of an inch (0.03 mm), capillaries are not much wider than a single red blood cell. This means they can run close to the cells of the body's tissues. When the blood leaves the capillaries, it flows into the veins and back to the heart.

Fast and Slow

Blood races along your arteries, pumped along by the heart muscle. By the time your blood has worked its way through the capillaries and back to the veins, it is moving much more slowly. The slow movement, together

How blood circulates around your body. Your heart is at the center and the main blood vessels reach every part of your body.

with the force of **gravity**, would make the blood pool in the long veins of your legs if these veins didn't lie between muscles. When these muscles tighten, they help to squeeze the blood back to the heart.

Thin Walls

The walls of the capillaries are just one cell thick so that nutrients and gases can pass easily between the blood and every cell in the body's tissues. **Glucose** and oxygen flow into the cells, while carbon dioxide and other waste material pass back into the blood.

Did You Know?

The blood vessels in an adult placed end to end would reach almost five times around the world!

Soldiers need to tense and relax their calf muscles when they stand still for a long time. If they don't, they may faint because blood can pool in their leg veins and reduce the blood flow to the brain.

Understanding How Blood Circulates

Dr. William Harvey (1578–1657) was the first person to show that blood circulates around the body and that the heart is a pump that keeps the blood moving. He also explained how the **valves** in the veins work to make sure that blood keeps flowing in one direction.

Arteries and Veins

Arteries and veins are specially designed to carry blood. Your arteries carry blood rich in oxygen away from the heart under high pressure. Your veins carry blood that has lots of carbon dioxide back to the heart under much lower pressure.

Arteries Versus Veins

All arteries have muscular and elastic walls. The strength and stretchiness helps them to cope with the high pressure of the blood pumped around your body by your heart. But the walls of most arteries are only about $^1/_{25}$ inch (1 mm) thick.

Veins don't need to carry blood at high pressure, so they have thin stretchy walls. Some of them, such as the long veins in the legs, have valves in them. These valves make sure that the slow-moving blood continues traveling back to the heart, even if this means flowing upwards against gravity.

One Exception

Arteries always carry blood rich in oxygen and veins always carry blood that has little oxygen, but there is one exception to this rule. When blood flows between the heart and the lungs, the pulmonary arteries carry blood with little oxygen from the heart to the lungs and

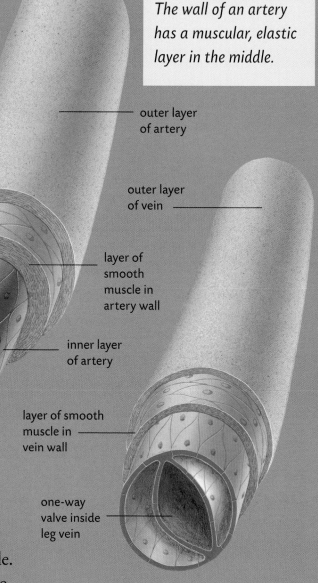

The wall of an artery has a muscular, elastic layer in the middle.

outer layer of artery

outer layer of vein

layer of smooth muscle in artery wall

inner layer of artery

layer of smooth muscle in vein wall

one-way valve inside leg vein

A leg vein has a one-way valve that stops blood from pooling in the feet.

the pulmonary veins ferry blood with lots of oxygen back to the heart.

Changing Flow

The smallest arteries are called **arterioles**, and they take blood to the capillaries. There are hundreds of millions of arterioles around our bodies and they have a very important role: they can widen (dilate) or narrow (constrict) to adjust the amount of blood that flows to each tissue or organ.

Veins and arteries can also dilate and constrict to send blood where your body most needs it. When you run, your leg muscles need more blood,

The skin of your face and other parts of your body turns red as your blood gets rid of some heat when you exercise.

but when you eat, your stomach needs more blood to deliver the fuel your body needs.

If all your blood vessels dilated at the same time, there wouldn't be enough blood to go around your whole circulatory system! So when some vessels dilate, others must constrict.

A Powerful Pump

Your heart is amazing. Its muscular walls pump blood to every part of your body, right down to the tips of your toes, without taking a rest for your whole life. Your beating heart speeds up when you run or are frightened, yet it always returns to a normal, steady rhythm.

Four Chambers

Your heart lies under your ribs between your lungs, just to the left of the breastbone. Its walls are made of muscle, called cardiac muscle. Inside there are four sections called chambers, with a valve linking each to control the flow of **blood** (see pages 18–19). The two chambers at the top are called the left **atrium** and the right atrium, and the two chambers at the bottom are called the left and right **ventricle**. These ventricles at the bottom are larger and stronger than the atria at the top because they do most of the pumping.

Your heart is made of thick muscle and is about the size of your fist. The muscle has its own supply of blood. This is brought by coronary arteries and taken away by coronary veins.

One Pump

Millions of branching muscle fibers in the walls of the four chambers work together to form one pump. These strong fibers **contract** and relax to make the heart beat and to drive the blood through the heart and then out into the body again via the aorta. Unlike the skeletal muscles elsewhere in your body,

aorta

blood to lungs

blood from lungs

coronary artery

coronary vein

An X-ray called a coronary angiogram shows the arteries that bring blood to the heart's muscle.

Heart Attack

Fatty substances can collect on the lining of coronary arteries in adults. This makes the arteries narrower. A blood clot can form nearby and block an artery altogether so that no blood reaches part of the heart muscle. This is what happens during a heart attack.

Muscle fibers are closely packed and contract together when the heart beats.

the fibers in the heart muscle are able to contract and relax on their own—and they do it about 100,000 times a day.

Blood for Your Heart

Your heart pumps blood all over your body, but the heart muscle needs its own supply of blood too. Blood full of oxygen and glucose is carried by a network of arteries that branch off the aorta, which is the body's biggest artery. These arteries are called the coronary arteries. They spread out over the surface of the heart. Veins run alongside the arteries and carry the blood away once the oxygen has been used by the heart muscle.

Flowing through the Heart

Your blood flows on a one-way journey through the two chambers on the right side of the heart and on to the lungs. From the lungs, it flows to the left side of the heart before setting off on its long trip around the body.

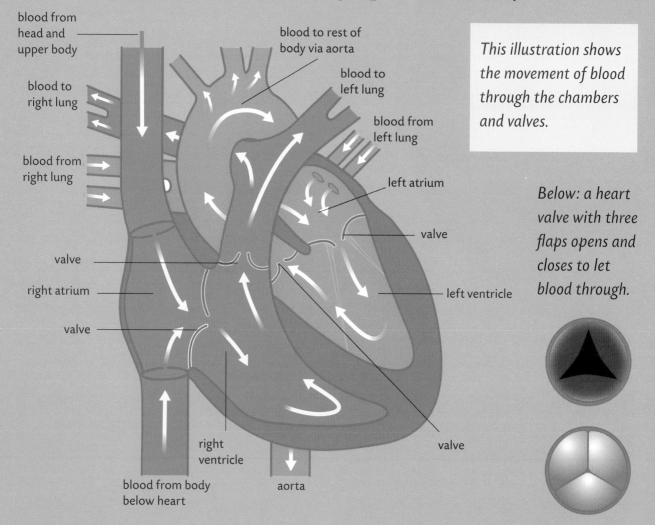

blood from head and upper body

blood to right lung

blood from right lung

valve

right atrium

valve

right ventricle

blood from body below heart

aorta

blood to rest of body via aorta

blood to left lung

blood from left lung

left atrium

valve

left ventricle

valve

This illustration shows the movement of blood through the chambers and valves.

Below: a heart valve with three flaps opens and closes to let blood through.

Two Sides

The heart has two sides—left and right— divided by a thick wall called the septum. The right atrium receives blood from the body and squeezes it into the right ventricle. This pumps the blood along the pulmonary arteries to the lungs where it picks up oxygen. Oxygen-rich blood from the lungs travels along the pulmonary veins and into the left atrium, which forces it into the left ventricle. The left ventricle has the thickest and most powerful walls of all the chambers because it has to pump blood along the aorta and around the body's vast network of blood vessels.

Heart Valves

Valves at the exit of each chamber keep the blood flowing in the right direction. Each valve has two or three flaps. When the muscular walls of a heart chamber contract, these flaps are forced apart and blood surges through. The pressure of the blood then pushes back on the flaps so they close again.

Before You Are Born

A baby in its mother's womb has different circulation because it doesn't use its lungs. Oxygen and other nutrients come through the umbilical cord (see pages 4-5). Blood carrying lots of oxygen from the placenta passes into the right side of the baby's heart. Most of it flows to the left side of the heart through a hole. From here, it is pumped into the aorta.

Once a baby is born and takes a breath of air, its lungs start to work. Then all the baby's blood flows to the lungs along the pulmonary arteries and back to the heart along the pulmonary veins.

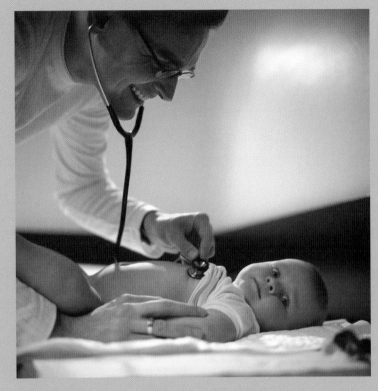

A doctor listens to a baby's beating heart through a stethoscope. The doctor can tell if there is a problem with the way the heart's valves open and close by how it sounds.

WHEN THINGS GO WRONG

The Sound of a Heart

When a doctor listens to your heart with a stethoscope, he or she hears two sounds —one after the other—as the valves of the heart close. The sound they make is "lub dup." If a heart valve is leaky or doesn't open properly, the doctor will hear an extra sound—this is called a heart murmur.

A Regular Beat

An adult's heart beats about 70 times every minute and about three billion times over a lifetime. What keeps our hearts beating tirelessly for the whole of our lives? The answer is a group of muscle cells in the wall of your heart.

Keeping Steady

The group of special muscle cells is in the wall of the right atrium in the top part of your heart (see pages 18–19). The cells keep the pace of your heart steady by sending tiny electric currents across the heart muscle. These regular and rhythmic currents spread across the upper chambers, making their muscle walls contract. They then spread to the two ventricles—the lower parts of your heart. So the muscles of the atria contract first, followed by the muscles of the ventricles. All this happens in less than a second!

Your Heartbeat

This sequence of contractions is the first stage of a heartbeat. This is when the heart sends blood to the body and to the lungs. During the second stage, the heart muscle relaxes and the chambers of the heart refill with blood from the body and the lungs.

First the right atrium and left atrium contract, then the right and left ventricles.

electric currents from muscle cells

blood into left ventricle

electric currents from muscle cells

blood into aorta

blood into right ventricle

blood to lungs

electric current

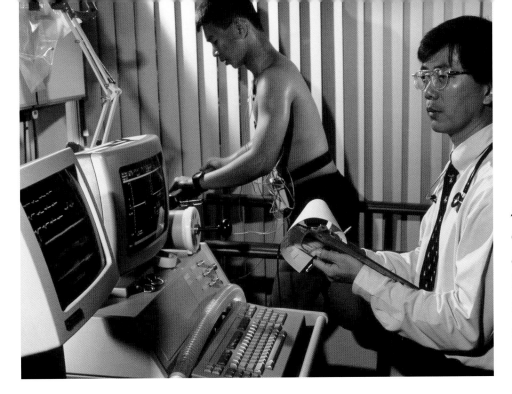

A man exercises on a machine while a doctor watches how his heart is working on two computer screens.

Faster and Slower

About 100 tiny electrical currents are sent out every minute. This rate speeds up or slows down if your body needs more or less oxygen and nutrients. For example, when you exercise or if you are afraid, your heart rate increases, and when you are resting or sleeping, your heart rate slows down.

Your heart rate usually changes when signals from the brain make the special muscle cells in the atrium send more or fewer electric currents to the heart muscle. Sometimes, hormones change your heart rate—for example, **adrenaline** speeds up heart contractions when you are excited or frightened. An adult's heart can beat 200 times a minute during exercise. The heart can also strengthen and weaken the force of the contractions, which changes the amount of blood it pumps out.

HEALTH CHECK
Taking Your Pulse

A doctor or nurse measures your heart rate by taking your pulse. Every time your heart contracts to squeeze blood along the arteries, there is a surge of blood and you can feel this by touching an artery that is close to the skin. Most of your arteries are too deep within the body to feel, but at the wrist the artery lies very near the surface over bone, so you can feel it easily.

Blood Pressure

Your body carefully controls the pressure of the blood flowing through your arteries. If your blood pressure is too high, it can damage organs such as your heart, brain, and kidneys, as well as blood vessels. If it is too low, parts of your body may not get enough blood.

Controlling Blood Pressure

Your blood pressure is controlled by your nervous system and by some hormones. The nervous system reacts very quickly when your blood pressure changes. It sends messages to the arteries to make them wider or narrower. It also sends messages to the heart to change how quickly it beats and how much blood it squeezes out when it contracts. Together, these adjustments bring blood pressure back to the right level.

Hormones are the body's chemical messengers. One or two hormones can

People can easily faint in a hot, crowded place such as a music festival.

Fainting

If your blood pressure suddenly falls too low and less blood flows to your brain, you could briefly lose consciousness. Fainting like this is common and lasts only a minute or two. It can be caused by many things, such as being stressed or standing in a hot, crowded place for a long time.

control blood pressure slowly over a few hours, mainly by changing the width of the arteries and adjusting the amount of fluid the kidneys pass out.

Measuring Pressure

When someone takes your blood pressure, they wrap a cuff around your upper arm. A stethoscope and timer are used to measure the heartbeats. A blood pressure measurement is made up of two numbers. The first is the pressure when the heart contracts and the second is the measurement when the heart relaxes and refills. The normal numbers for an adult's blood pressure are around 120 and 80. These numbers may be shown as 120/80.

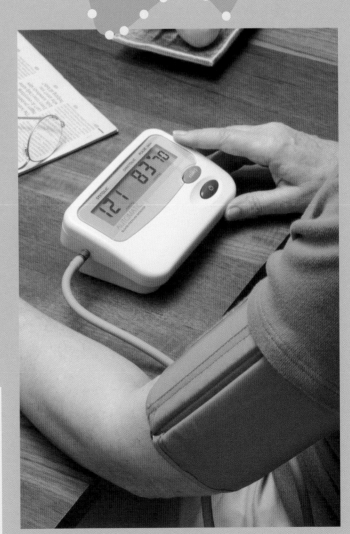

Machines are also used to measure blood pressure. A cuff is used and a digital monitor displays the two numbers.

Cleaning Your Blood

Two parts of your body clean your blood—your liver and your lungs. They have other vital jobs, too, such as taking nutrients from food (the liver) and adding oxygen to your blood (the lungs). If your liver and lungs did not keep taking harmful substances from your blood, you would die.

Your Amazing Liver

The liver is the largest organ in your body, and it does an incredible number of jobs. When your stomach takes in nutrients and chemicals, they enter the bloodstream and go straight to the liver in a vein called the portal vein. The liver sorts out useful substances and stores them. It also removes unwanted or harmful substances. Here are just a few of the things the liver removes:

- bilirubin, a chemical made when hemoglobin from red cells is broken down;

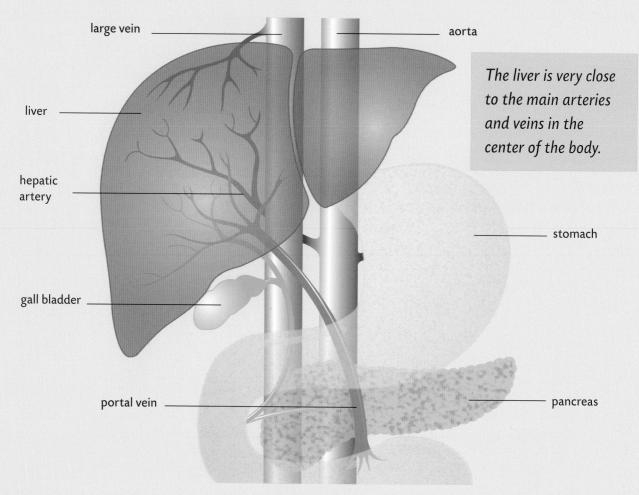

large vein

aorta

liver

The liver is very close to the main arteries and veins in the center of the body.

hepatic artery

stomach

gall bladder

portal vein

pancreas

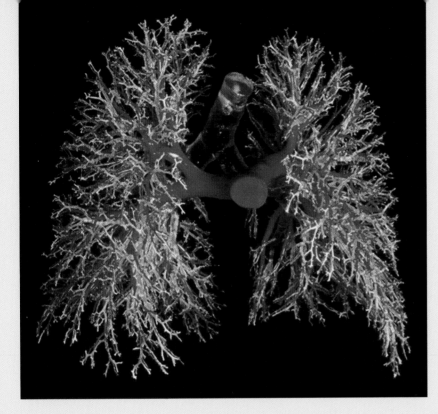

A model of the lungs shows the network of arterial blood vessels (red) and air passages (amber and white).

- alcohol, which has to be processed or it can damage the tissues—drinking too much alcohol can damage the liver;
- medicines, which need to be processed and gotten rid of as soon as they have done their job in the body;
- poisons and **toxins** that have entered the blood from your intestines or are created by an illness; these must be dealt with quickly to stop them from damaging body tissues.

Getting Rid of Carbon Dioxide

Carbon dioxide can be poisonous if it builds up in your blood. Your body gets rid of it by breathing it out of the lungs. The lungs contain large tubes (airways) that divide into smaller and smaller airways. These end in tiny sacs shaped like grapes, called **alveoli**, which are full of air. These tiny sacs have a huge surface area which can take in oxygen and give out carbon dioxide.

Did You Know?

An adult has around 600 million alveoli. If you flattened them all out into a sheet it would cover an area roughly the size of a tennis court.

The walls of alveoli are only one cell thick and they are covered in tiny, thin-walled blood capillaries. Gases can pass through them easily, so the unwanted carbon dioxide waste from our body cells goes into the air in our lungs and out of our bodies as we breathe out.

Passing through Filters

Your kidneys help to make sure you have the right amount of water and chemicals inside your body. They filter your blood, saving what your body needs and getting rid of (excreting) waste and unwanted water. These are stored in your bladder before passing out of the body as urine.

Two Small Organs

As well as keeping the right water levels in the body, the kidneys make hormones. These help to keep your blood pressure at the right level. The kidneys work hard despite their size—they each weigh little more than 3.5 ounces (100 g).

Tiny Filtering Units

Both kidneys contain millions of tiny filtering units called nephrons. Together, they filter your blood all day, every day. Each nephron sucks some water, salts, and minerals out of your blood and sends them down into a long, twisty tube as urine.

What's in the urine changes all the time as it passes along each tube. A network of blood vessels around each tube takes back some of the water and nutrients and more unwanted substances go from the blood into the urine. The urine flows into bigger and bigger tubes, and finally leaves the kidney in a tube called the ureter, which goes to the bladder.

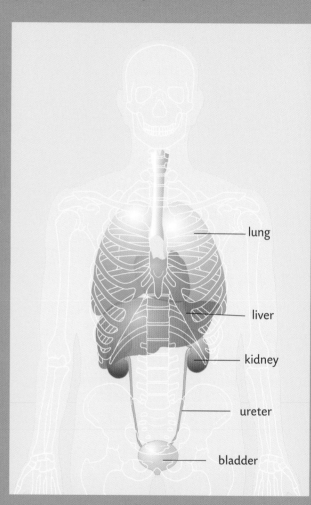

The two kidneys are at the back of the abdomen. The bladder sits in the middle of the pelvis.

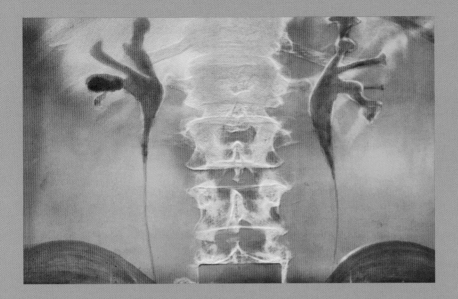

An X-ray of two kidneys shows that a stone has formed in one (see red area on far left). Substances in urine can form stones that may cause a blockage.

A cross section through a kidney shows how urine runs into the ureter.

How a Nephron Works

blood from renal artery

water, salts, and minerals taken from blood

some water, salts, and minerals return to blood

blood flow

urine in tube

millions of nephrons

renal artery

millions of urine tubes

ureter

Did You Know?

Your kidneys receive lots of blood delivered at high speed—all your blood passes through your kidneys at least 300 times every day.

Water on the Move

An adult usually passes between four to eight cups (1–2 L) of urine every day. Once the kidneys have made urine, it is stored in the bladder before passing out of the body. Our nervous system sends messages when we need to urinate, but it also makes sure that we can wait until we are ready.

Storing Urine

An adult's stretchy bladder can hold about two cups (0.5 L) of urine. When you need to urinate, nerve signals go to the spinal cord, which sends signals back to the bladder with instructions to contract and squeeze the urine out through the urethra. To make sure that you urinate at the right times, your brain also sends messages that control when you pass urine.

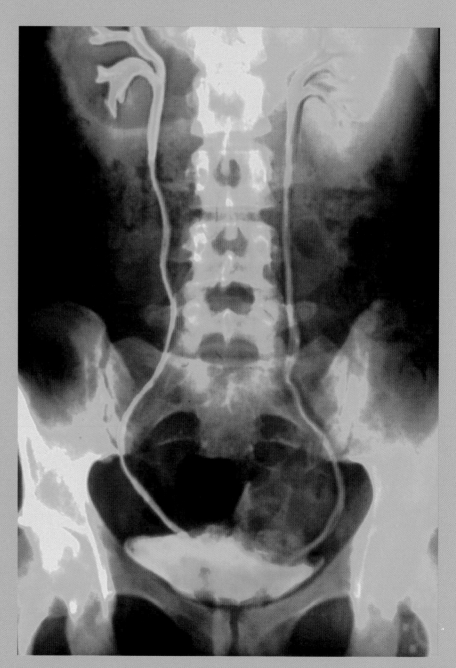

This X-ray shows the two kidneys at the top, and the two ureters leading down to the bladder inside the pelvis.

What Is Urine?

Urine is around 95 percent water. The rest is unwanted substances and waste dissolved in the water. These include salts, waste from the muscles, and urea, which is produced when **proteins** are broken down. After it leaves the body, urine can start to smell. This is because bacteria break down the urea and produce ammonia, which can have a foul smell. When urine contains lots of water, it is a pale straw color. Concentrated urine is a much darker color. The color of our urine can be affected by what we eat—for example, if you eat beets it can make your urine red!

HEALTH CHECK
Testing Urine

Testing urine is a way of checking for signs of certain illnesses. Protein in urine can be the sign of a urinary tract infection (UTI). If urine has a lot of sugar in it, this may point to diabetes (problems with controlling the amount of sugar in the blood). Blood in the urine may be caused by a bladder or kidney problem. Special testing sticks are dipped in urine. They change color depending on what is in the urine.

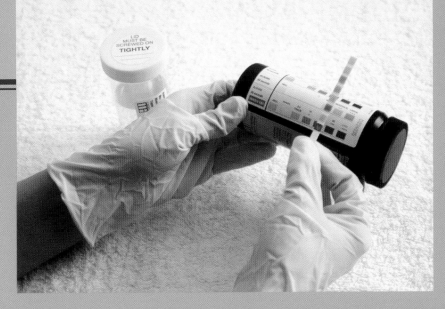

A testing stick that has been dipped in urine is held next to a container showing the range of colors it might match.

Glossary

adrenaline   A hormone from the adrenal glands that speeds up breathing and heart rate.

alveoli   Tiny air sacs in the lungs where oxygen enters the blood and carbon dioxide leaves the blood.

anemia   An illness that makes someone tired because they can't carry enough oxygen in their blood.

aorta   The large artery carrying blood away from the heart.

arteriole   A small artery carrying blood to the capillaries.

artery   A blood vessel that takes blood from the aorta and carries it to the arterioles.

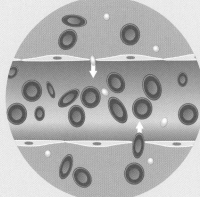

atrium   An upper chamber in the heart. The right atrium receives blood from the body and the left atrium from the lungs.

bilirubin   A chemical produced when hemoglobin is broken down.

blood pressure   The pressure of the blood against the walls of the arteries.

bone marrow   A jelly-like substance inside the bones.

capillary   A tiny blood vessel that carries blood to the cells of the body.

clot   Blood that has thickened into a lump.

contraction   The shortening of the fibers in a muscle.

donor   Someone who gives an organ, such as a kidney, or a tissue, such as bone marrow, to an ill person who needs it to live.

glucose   A simple sugar that the body's cells need for generating energy.

gravity   The force that pulls everything toward the center of the Earth.

hemoglobin   A large protein that carries oxygen in the blood.

hormone   One of the chemicals that act as messengers in the body. Hormones help control the way the body works and develops.

nervous system   The body's communications system. Nerves in the brain, spinal cord, and the rest of the body continually send electrical messages to help control the way the body works.

nutrient   One of many chemicals the body needs to live. Nutrients include carbohydrates, proteins, fats, vitamins, and minerals.

organ   A major part of the body that has one or more special tasks. The heart, lungs, liver, kidneys, eyes, and ears are all organs.

plasma   The pale yellow liquid in your blood.

platelet   A tiny scrap of a cell in the blood.

protein   A chemical that is essential for cells to grow and work.

spleen   An organ near the stomach that breaks down red blood cells and makes white blood cells, especially in newborn babies.

stethoscope   A medical instrument used by medical staff to listen to the sounds from a patient's heart.

toxin   A chemical that can poison the body if it is not removed or broken down.

valve   Flaps of tough tissue in the heart or leg veins that let blood through in one direction only.

ventricle   A lower chamber in the heart. The right ventricle pumps blood to the lungs while the left pumps blood into the aorta.

Further Reading

Levete, Sarah. *Understanding the Heart, Lungs, and Blood* (Understanding the Human Body) Rosen Central, 2010.

Lew, Kristi. *Clot & Scab : Gross Stuff about Your Scrapes, Bumps, and Bruises* (Gross Body Science) Millbrook Press, 2010.

Walker, Denise. *Cells and Life Processes* (Basic Biology) Smart Apple Media, 2007.

Web Sites

www.kidsbiology.com/ human_biology/circulatory-system3.php
Explore the circulatory system.

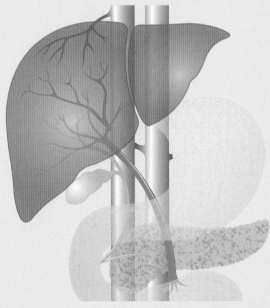

www.fi.edu/learn/heart/index.html
Find out about how the heart develops and works, how doctors monitor it, and how to keep it healthy.

Index